MUSINGS OF THE WISTFUL GENTLEMAN (AND OTHER PERSONALITIES)

A collection of poetry

Written and illustrated by

CARENZA ELIZABETH GREED
(AKA 'Wren')

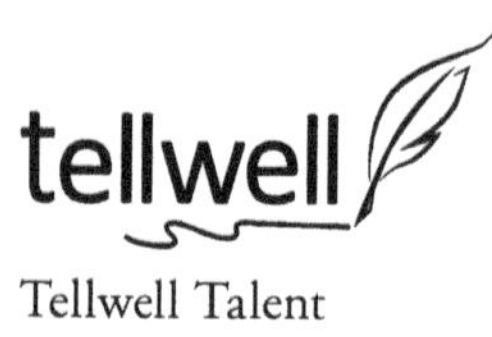

Tellwell Talent
www.tellwell.ca

ISBN
978-1-77962-718-6 (Paperback)

PREFACE

Musings of the wistful gentleman (and other personalities) is a semi autobiographical piece of work by Carenza Elizabeth Greed that explores personal experiences with gender, addiction, grief, mental illness, religion and the occult and existential pondering. Carenza compares themselves to 'the wistful gentleman' on the back cover, showing the representation they feel best matches their internal self, despite the presentation of their outward appearance. This is author Carenza Elizabeth Greed's first book.

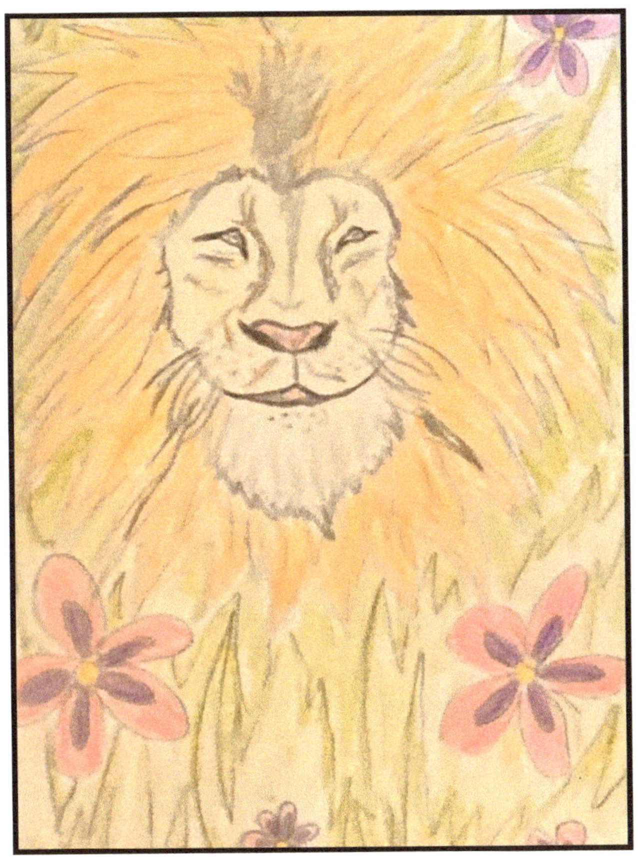

ABOUT THE AUTHOR

Carenza Elizabeth Greed grew up and has lived their life so far in Brighton in the southeast of England. They attended a C of E primary until the age of 11 and despite gaps in their education due to lifelong struggles with mental health conditions, achieved an access course in their early 20's and went on to attend university studying psychology. Psychology is an important part of their life due to their own struggles and they live with the hope that one day they can use their experiences to help other people suffering from mental health conditions. Carenza's artistic side was always present throughout their childhood, whereby they loved to write and was told by a teacher that they 'used words like an artist'. In their 'tween' years they enjoyed film making and directed and edited movies as often as they were able to. In their late teens they tried out modelling and completed a few shoots and videos; they also wrote lyrics and sung in a series of songs which they got produced which to their own admission weren't 'very good' but just another way for their artistic side to emerge. Carenza is a vegan of ten years and enjoys nature, taking opportunities such as their gardening volunteering job that they had in 2024 at the historical properties 'Anne of Cleves' house and 'Lewes Castle', both in Lewes, East Sussex. Despite the many challenges they have faced in their life due to mental ill health they remain resilient even in the darkest of times and aim to connect with others through their art.

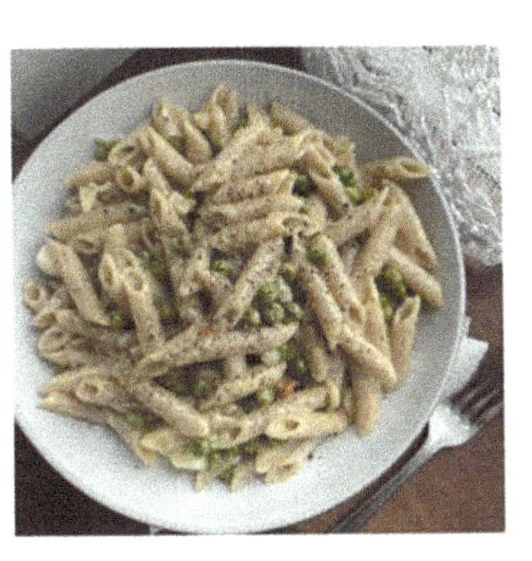

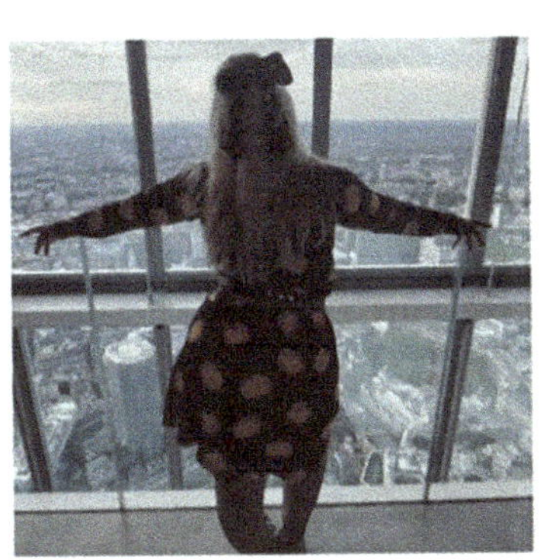

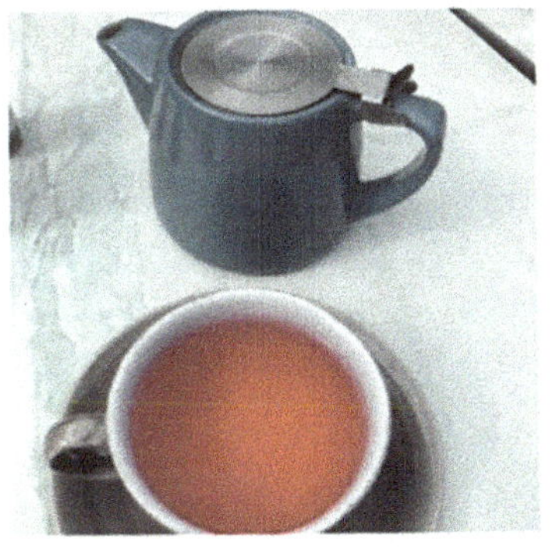

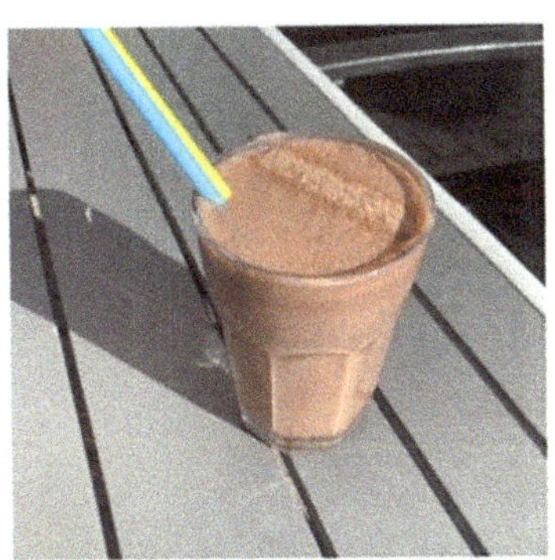

~Dedicated to all those lost in the last few years~

Dear reader, keep love true in your heart. Have the courage and bravery of a knight and the roar of a lion; have the swiftness of a sparrow and agility of a gazelle. Don't let the world tear you apart, and remain good and well.

TABLE OF CONTENTS

The lake

Across a lake I cast my gaze,
Amidst the muskgrass and the haze.
The bleak serenity of despair,
A peaceful place, the clean wet air.
I hear a bird up over head,
And wonder to why here i'm lead;
Whenever sadness takes its root,
Inside I cry and yet stay mute.
Oh what a sight I do behold,
Unlike a story ever told.
I smile and think, 'what calm, what storm!',
And thus another poet's born.
"Dichotomous, the rest and wake;
Death and life, my mind, the lake."

Pastry shop

The taste of sugar on my lips,
A pastry shop where people sit,
Outside when weather is permissive,
Friendly folk with smiles emissive.
The wind is slight but not a bother,
And oh! The people, ever proper.
A place where one must be polite,
But Lord knows what goes on at night.
The pastry, though, is quite a treat.
Then to my office I'll retreat.
I'll finish what is left of work,
'But not quite now I think' I smirk.
For what sport else, which passes time,
Has pastries, tea and clementines?
My favourite spot is here, I say!
The light relief within each day.
Time moves on with gentle leisure,
My soul knows weight, but also pleasure.

The gamble

A war of politicians grit,
Where sword-like tongues are requisite.
In life we must but overcome,
All for glory or all for none.
You moved your chess piece,
I moved mine.
Strategies that intertwine.
But what to choose,
Which step to take,
What does a good leader make?
Sacrifices must be made,
Opponent sharpening his blade.
There's nothing but the final go,
The callousness, the final blow.
Every man thinks he shall win,
A gamble made by fools in sin.
A gentleman until the end,
I'll shake his hand just like a friend.
But inside we have cruel intent,
One can win, none will repent.
A duel of jokers, seeking power,
Desolate, the final hour.

Wife

I sit in silent contemplation,
Marvelling at your creation.
And was it not for Gods or stars,
We would not be here where we are.
Your beauty is a fiery blaze,
Bold and fierce your emerald gaze.
A woman who has weathered storms,
A shapeshifter with many forms.
And here I am, the lucky man.
The one that gets to hold your hand.
The one who kneels and bears a ring.
And with one word, my heart does sing.
So when I walk you down the aisle,
I'll do so with a nervous smile.
The future is the great unknown,
But since we met I've changed, I've grown.
Now I have nothing to fear,
You see, I'll be with you my dear.

Red romance

Oh song! I cry. Oh symphony!
To have you here right next to me.
Vivaldi plays and angels dance.
Heralding our red romance.
My collar sits a bit too tight,
Undo a button; there's too much light.
I'm nervous but you're calm as ever,
As though my lungs are made of leather.
Rasping breaths, your gentle laugh,
We bathe in lights, oh what a bath.
Tonight will be our consummation,
Already I feel exaltation.
You see, a man like me is shy,
And when you look me in the eye,
I feel my body start to tremble.
Can we switch to light by candle?
You lean in slow and touch my face,
I'm reassured by your embrace.
Your satin dress against my skin,
My senses make this feel like sin.
And yet we are now bound by God,
And so the feeling's rather odd.
A pleasure that is mounting high,
My fingertips against your thigh.
Your lipstick stains against my neck,
I say a prayer, for I'm a wreck.
Our first of many blissful nights,
My love! An angel clad in white.
My fire! My Star! My feathered grace!
I see my future in your face.

Alien

Starlight; fragile specs of dust,
Illuminated and forward thrust.
Lime green skin and clad in gold,
A sci-fi from the days of old.
Buy seeds, plant!
Buy seeds, sow!
They won't survive against the snow.
Spaceship engine, clouds of smoke,
Pollution seeping into oak.
Extravagance and opal jewels,
A brand new era, brand new rules.
Alien in all but song,
We wonder where it all went wrong.
Reflections of a long dead world,
The mirrors tremble, shake the clouds.
Falling sleet, my unmade bed,
Whispers permeate my head.
Oh how it suffers! How it moans!
Scattered thoughts and painful groans.
Planets shiver, knocked off course.
And who are we? Why, we're the source.

Wistful gentleman

Oh what a fool, this wistful man.
For all these years without a plan,
And all the paths that I have tread,
Well sir, you see just where they've led.
With my pipe of fine tobacco,
Analysing this fiasco.
What a fool calls himself Sire?
Driven by infernal fire.
My golden locks and lace up boots,
My velvet suit, my smugglers loot.
I've lived a life that dripped with pain,
So long as I could keep my reign.
And now the journey nears its end,
I reminisce on foes and friends.
Nostalgic of the better times,
The love…The fine imported wine!
There's been some highs, and low's a plenty.
I've graced this time, this honoured century.
With this breath, for it may be my last,
I signed this book, 'Here lies my past'.

Wolves

When feelings are there, feelings will no doubt be hurt.
Like a sharp knife in amongst a rainstorm,
Where there's no sanctuary from the relentless tirade of misery.
And there you were, love at first sight.
The days became torture, I lived in the nights.
I lived in a fantasy of pure bliss.
Imagining the soft touch of your lips.
And meanwhile, I was in danger, a pack of wolves surrounding me.
You grounded me.
But you didn't want me and I was left as prey.
Now nothing can keep the darkness away.

Chess

I can see it playing out in slow motion,
Every turn only becomes clear seconds after the piece is moved.
That painful feeling that lends itself to romanticising.
The sapphire teardrops that fall onto the board as the winner is
    eventually announced.
The game is over before checkmate.
It's clear who the winner will be and any attempt to save face is long
    gone.
You had the winning hand, the power, the practice.
I had a weeping heart and a lack of clarity.
I congratulate you and we shake hands,
But you take the win as a certainty,
I took the loss as a crushing blow.

Beauty

I appreciate beauty,
Carved marble statues and one of a kind paintings from a period far
  more tasteful.
I appreciate classical music and notes so perfect they delight the
  senses.
The crisp winter air,
The soft summer sand.
Luxury,
Elegance,
Decadence.
I appreciate beauty.

Grief

I see your face in every stranger,
I freeze as though I am in danger,
It's like a shock takes over me,
A rush of pain and guilt and grief.
It's been a year but feels like more,
Ignoring wounds that remain sore.
Since I was told what had become,
Of someone who's life had just begun.
I've downed my thoughts, destroyed my brain,
Couldn't take the endless pain.
How do you mourn when you're at fault?
I could have been there but I did nought.
In fact I see the part I played,
A person who helped lead you astray.

To which I overheard in the tavern

'In my darkest hour, I cower, alone.
The moon shines so brightly,
The stars feel like home.
Pretending there's arms that hold me tight.
Delusions that I'm not alone in this night.
I don't even wish now for someone who cares,
You can use me, abuse me, I've gone past despair.
Just keep me company, that is enough,
Distract me, confuse me, be vague or be tough.
Just keep me from feeling as lonely as this,
I'd do almost anything, I'd take every risk.
I'd do any substance, I'd drink any drink,
I'd lay under strangers rather than think.
Befriending bottles, or powder or lies,
Tolerating men who slip between my thighs.
I feel like I'm hollow, there's nothing that's *me*.
There's only the void there where I used to be.'

The rush

There's been a void, an emptiness.
The world was at a standstill.
No taste or colour or vibrancy,
I couldn't seem to feel.
And then, for you, came flooding in,
Of all the things that life can bring.
I felt the rush and suddenly,
My heart had started, jolting me.
I couldn't sleep, I couldn't eat,
Counting down the days.
Every moment I'm with you's a moment that I crave.
But we cant be, so what a trick,
The cruellest hand of fate.
I met the one who saved me but I met them just too late.
They're happy and they are in love,
Like church bells and a flock of doves.
And what of me? What am I now?
A zombie hastened back to life?
Only to be happy then to walk into a knife.
I didn't know that I could love,
I gave up quite completely,
'It's better to have loved and lost',
But now this blow has beat me.
The pain's too much to tolerate,
To picture what could be.
Because you will still have those things,
But they won't be with me.

The womb

Stop leaving the house,
Stop waking up,
The cheapest wine to fill my cup.
My life gets smaller,
Wall's closing in,
Deliberately, from here to fin.
Disappear,
Who am I?
Destroy my personality.
Replace it with pure nothingness,
It's better than insanity.
What do I like?
I have no hobbies,
I have no talents,
My will is wobbly.
And even still there's too much there,
I still wake up,
Still think, still care.
If only I had never left,
The womb or if I could return,
To cease to exist,
To vanish,
To be put into an urn.
I never asked for this to be,
To live or to be born.
And now it is,
Somewhere between,
Death and life,
See I am torn.

Oh, spring!

Sweet floral breeze, the cobblestone path,
The flirting of the coming spring.
Wonder, history and calm,
You catch yourself starting to sing.
It feels a time of optimism,
A moment where things start to change,
There's hope amongst the blooming life,
Suddenly you're feeling strange.
It is as if the world around,
Is offering a friendly hand,
It says, 'you had to go through this'.
As if life has a greater plan.
Butterflies will soon emerge,
The sun will gain it's glowing heat,
It is a period of growth,
A tradition that yearly repeats.
Oh spring! Good morning,
It is a pleasure,
Memories are dancing now,
The green man throws the petals,
Pan concludes it with a bow.

Half way house for souls

At this half way house for souls,
The people rest, they all decay.
Sitting on their hope as if they'll be a rainy day;
Upon which they can spend it but the summer brings a drought.
And years and decades pass and then,
They still reside here with nought.
At this halfway house for souls,
The people are robotic,
Going through the motions as if they are hypnotic.
Riding on a roller coaster that will never end,
Not stopping once to check the time,
Restrained, they cannot bend.
The sand runs out, the wrinkles crease,
And for a second the silence ceased.
And all at once the wasted youth,
The years of running from the truth.
They never took a chance or leap,
Not recalling how to move their feet.
This limbo of the lifeless ones,
The person I fear I'll become.

Lucifer

When you close your eyes,
He's the light that you see through your lids.
A white glow in utter darkness.
Both the sun and the moon,
The night and the day.
He's both a lighthouse in a storm,
And the one who commands it.
A trickster and a poet,
A lover albeit possessive.
Calm but furious,
Guiding yet rocking your way.
The devil and an angel.
My love, my love.

Handkerchief

When I pull out my handkerchief,
And give it to you,
It reminds me of my youth,
And the times I was blue.
My father carried one,
And whenever I'd weep,
He'd give me a handkerchief,
In which tears would seep.
It made me feel better,
I can't explain how,
But It's strange how these things,
Seem nostalgic now.
I carry my own now wherever I go,
And it reassures me from sadness or woe.
My dear this is something,
That's been on my mind,
The past and those moments,
Of comfort I'd find.

Butterfly

Oh wings of paper,
Flutter, please!
Symphonies across the breeze.
The lantern's on,
The lake runs warm,
It's evening now,
And what a swarm!
Oh, how it's nice to see your life,
Your existence, devoid of strife.
Antenna pointed at the moon,
Reflection of you in my spoon.
A whisper comes,
But just for me,
One day, like them, you will be free.

The barrel

Roll the barrel, ever steady,
Down the hill, the content's heavy.
And what a man or what a wit,
Would build a space where you can fit,
A paragraph of ill design,
And may it rest, the words resign.
For if I were to speak them out,
Those raging screams i'm numb without;
I fear contemporaries views,
They'd see a man, a mouse, a muse.
But also they would see a ghost,
Who drinks the doubts he fears the most.
The crashing waves of melancholy,
In amongst his inventory.
The cries, the shrill and piercing screams,
The nightmares stealing all his dreams,
With outward facades holding tight,
Composure of an honoured knight.
Within decay has taken seat,
The rotting of the tortured meat.
And with this barrel I dispose,
Of secrets, ensure no one knows.
That I am dying deep within,
A man of pain, of ghouls, of sin.

Antique

I spent my time loving you,
Just like people do.
For we all give our hearts,
Not once, but often.
And you are most loyal,
To those whom you treasure,
I suppose I am a thing of the past.
But like all antiques,
I can be repurposed.
And so from the dust,
I rise, I rise.

Human

I chased the ultimate beauty,
When a lesser demon would do.
For it seems I was wrong,
In my pursuit of you.
I didn't find much happiness,
Or were it but illusion?
It seems the wool is off my eyes,
I have no more confusion.
I realise I am not unique,
That this thing happens every week;
To anyone that's anywhere,
To every soul that lives to care.
And I suppose that there is solace,
I know that I was open, honest.
I find my peace with that it's true,
It seems I'm human just like you.

Written in the sun

Goodbye my past,
I pull the blinds,
My future is awaiting.
I don't know where this road will lead,
But damn who cares?!
I'll make it.
I'll set out on this journey,
It was written in the sun,
This blonde haired man,
This man I am,
He's got a lot to come.
And oh, of course,
I'll make mistakes,
It's something that I count on.
But it's one step closer,
To my fate,
And who I will become.

Mortal

Wipe away those tears,
You're mortal and that hurts.
I'm sorry I've to tell you this,
But see it's not the worst.
You're flesh and bone,
You're fragile.
You'll bruise along the way.
You'll cry for people when they leave,
Begging them to stay.
You'll have times when you're all alone,
These moments, they will sting.
But you were put here on this earth,
For all the things you bring.
And yes you're not a hero,
Not in the sense you wish.
You'll never be a daring knight,
Who gets the maiden's kiss.
But you will do things so unique,
You're gonna leave your mark.
So pick yourself up right away,
As this is just the start.

Cautionary tale

Older, more worn,
Years have eluded me.
One concept persists,
One that's not new to me.
I am lazy, lax,
I do not excel.
It's all caught up,
Now all can tell.
With no medals, trophies,
Badges of honour;
Can't live by reflections I catch in the mirror.
I want more years,
I want a rerun.
But I'd end up doing,
Just what I have done.
In all of these years,
I have but tales,
Cautionary and going stale.
I wish to live through someone else,
They'd tell me it's a cry for help.
I never start but I will end,
Here lies a failure, a son, a friend.

Witches

The cauldron burns,
Smoke pervades the air,
On a cloudy evening,
Scent caught in my hair.
My cigarette lit,
Intentions clear,
The chime of bells,
Draw ever near.
The crows are screaming,
I am too.
I stare into the fire,
And in it there's you.
Halloween is but hours away,
For it is like no other day.
My spell burns quickly,
Turns to ashes.
Turning inwards,
Your eyelashes.
Count to three,
Just like they're wishes.
Now you know,
Don't mess with witches.

Ghost

In fear I hide and become trapped,
The darkness ever holds me back.
Fear of life and fear of death,
Fear that there is nothing left.
Fear of people, fear of me,
Fear of all I've come to be.
I'm terrified of even moving,
Can't master the art of self soothing.
It's not just superficial terror,
It's accumulated from what I've weathered.
A lasting stain from all I've seen,
The awful places I have been.
I mourn for innocence I lost,
For this appears to be the cost.
I weep for who I could be now,
If I had not walked right through hell.
A shadow of the man I knew,
And just another ghost to you.

Golden

Long await the shining.
The glimmer that was stolen.
For you were just like Midas,
With your touch so rich and golden.
Long await the time again,
In which we both do meet.
Strangers who at once do stop,
When passing on the street.
And there we stand and ponder,
The in's and out's of us.
The happy days, the sea breeze waves,
The tears, the broken trust.
Perhaps we'll go for coffee,
Cigarette in hand.
We'll laugh and things come flooding back,
You'll ask me, 'where'd we stand?'.
And then we'll fall in love again,
But this time it will last.
Because we miss the golden mist,
That was our troubled past.

Human kind

Our differences set us apart,
Preceding fighting from the start.
But there is more that bonds us see,
Abundant similarity.
States of mind or minds of state,
Blind-sighted by the hands of fate.
And ignorance in handfuls too,
But connected we are all to you.
And you to I, and I to they,
The bible has some truths to say.
For we are all in this together,
A pack, a group, birds of a feather.
So if we put aside the malice,
Built a structure like a palace,
Metaphoric sanctuary,
Where we live in harmony.
And we could achieve further knowledge,
A small mind just keeps you in bondage.
All together, all as one,
A new age of the people, come!
Stand together, stand united.
No longer confused or short sighted.
And we'll rise, the human kind.
So let's leave squabbling behind.

Live

Bellowing, the urgent cries,
Before another dear friend dies.
The shouting from inside my head,
In light of all that now are dead.
'Live!' it says. 'Really live!'
A calling from a higher source.
And this is all following on from,
A time of grief, of pain, remorse.
From this time on I will do better,
Be a better friend.
I had all but given up,
And that must now come to an end.
'Live!' I hear and now it seems,
The subconscious, perhaps my dreams,
Or dare I say direct from God,
Because this feeling's rather odd.
A parting gift or just my health,
But something is still screaming.
'Live a life that's full of love and hopefulness and meaning'.

Change

No longer will I spend my time,
Lost inside a glass.
I will not waste a single day,
Be gone my hopeless past!
If i'm alive then there's still time,
More words to fit into this rhyme.
More chances of redemption and,
For me to lend a helping hand.
If I've been given more to do,
Then I will do it all for you.
You'll be my muse and be my hope,
I'll never again hang a rope.
I'll never forget what I have,
The blessings in my life,
Perhaps the future holds a job,
Maybe I'll take a wife.
But all I know for certain now,
Is I will not stop fighting,
To make a change despite my chains,
I hope I do by writing.

Love

Life goes on, even when it doesn't.
Bindweed swallows up what's left of the house.
I can only surmise that in its cells is a part of you.
Even in winter, there are plants that thrive,
And every hour: another death, another new life.
A never ending cycle, replenishing lost stock.
Raining on the fields that gasp for moisture,
Growing, living, dying.
And all whilst we're crying. All whilst we're crying.
I don't know if we'll meet again,
I stand frozen in this life,
You in another.
Time is an illusion, many things are.
Never knowing which day the flower will be plucked from the earth.
Love, I say. Just be and just love.

Padded white rooms

You all love to hate me,
And hate that you love me.
We all like a bad boy you have to admit.
Without medication I fit the criteria,
For absolute madness,
Hysteria fits.

As of right now,
I seem i'm together,
Because I'm sedated, and under the weather.
Alas in my mind,
Chaos still reigns.
Only subdued by the chemical chains.

Feast on my splendour,
And where I was made,
My ancestors tortured,
In Bedlam, enslaved.
I share all their consciousness,
Feel all their wounds.
We all rock together,
In padded white rooms.

Me

Nobody knows me,
They may think they do from brief interactions.
They may see a gambling man, a drunk or a fiend.
They may see a man who has no future, a man who has no morals.
But this man, who sits and dwells, who behind closed doors writes
poems with classical music playing softly in the background;
The man who dreams and this man who cries.
The man who loses his sanity more each time someone dies.
I am multifaceted. Sometimes I am fierce, sometimes frail.
Sometimes I don't recognise myself in the mirror.
Sometimes I love myself entirely.
Always I see more than I let on, observe people in all their humanity
as well as my own.
My highs and my lows, my love and my fears.
My loyalty and my strength, the laughter, the tears.
There are twenty four hours in a day and all the men I am and were,
all the men I'm yet to become.
People's minds work as such that they take their interaction with you
as all you are and can be.
You don't know this man sir,
You just don't know me.

Hope

I'll be the one to save myself,
I locked up my own chains.
I threw away the key and I declared it was my reign.
A king of sorrow, king of tears,
Monarch of the worldly fears.
And somehow that was safer than,
If I'd allowed myself to dream.
You see if id have opened up,
I would have with a tortured scream.
Better to succumb to sorrow,
Than to hope for a better morrow.
But now I see I wasted years,
Enslaved by all my troubled fears.
But now I dare to think of more,
I can't predict the outcome.
I could be crushed and buried,
'Here lies a foolish son'.
Risky if my heart's not closed,
For then it could be broken.
But once it's there and once it's said,
Hope cannot be unspoken.

Firearm

Oh no Sir, don't you draw your gun,
As if you were the holy one.
As if you have a right to fire,
Every man thinks himself higher.
Oh tell me now, which thought you've had,
That's made you look this weak and sad?
Hath made you take on God himself,
And brewed this venom in your mouth.
'He deserves it'.
Justify;
Why from your hand a man should die.
Petty men with fleeting power,
Used to make the others cower.
'Oh my, isn't he so strong?'
Is that what girls say where you're from?
And is it because they're afraid,
When men are changed and monsters made?
But I won't play into your dream,
I will not tremble, will not scream.
I'm staring down the barrel now,
It's you, not I, who'll end up in hell.

Hell's gift

Rest your head against my chest,
I will always protect you.
You know I'm far from all the rest,
Of men you've become used to.
I may not love you like you wish,
I love the devil more.
But your forehead I will kiss,
It's you I do adore.
You see on journeys back from hell,
I'll bring with me a gift.
Your eyes light up, it's going swell,
But there's something that you missed.
While you are alone with me,
The devil claims you too.
And one day you will grow to see,
That like me, he loves you.

Piece

I don't just wanna live,
I don't just wanna die.
I wanna find out quickly,
All the reasons why.
Why this world is so cruel,
Why we are put through it.
Curiosity killed the cat,
But something's got to do it.
I wear my coat of silver coins,
That jingle when I move.
I wear a strong jaw with my pride,
They're things I've yet to prove.
I am one man, an army no,
It's lonely where I have to go.
But I try, and i'm sincere,
To say my piece whilst I am here.

Where we part

I see the line that separates us,
Etched into the bark.
Now here we shake hands,
Say farewell,
For this is where we part.
It's been so swell, I've no regrets,
I hope your journey's kind.
Between us no outstanding debts,
Or things we've yet to find.
I worry for you I must say,
My road looks far more safe.
But I know now as well as you,
We're destined to a place.
I cannot walk on by your side,
For I am on a mission.
But i'll tell of you to all I meet,
Or all that care to listen.
Dear friend we will still stay in touch,
Even if nought to share,
For we are different people now,
But I still truly care.

Eccentric

My poems are reflective,
I write just how I speak.
A deeper vulnerability,
You may mistake as weak.
I may not be so linear,
The lines may deviate;
From what is 'good and proper',
Oh it's a heavy weight.
You may misunderstand me,
Or think I am insane.
But I am just an artist,
Making things out of my pain.
I am an old romantic,
Imaginative fool,
Head in the clouds, can't touch the ground,
I forgot the first rule.
The lesson to be 'normal',
I must have been away;
For I have been eccentric,
Every single waking day.

Addiction for me is like giving birth

Everyone is hyped up by it,
It's fresh, it's new, it's exciting.
And the pain that follows, the waves of agony, the near death
experiences.
I'm fighting for my life, praying to God like there's no tomorrow,
begging for a second chance.
I'm worried that I won't ever see my mum again, my friends.
No life comes from it, just death. Death.
And it almost took me too.
Took my friends, walked me to their funerals.
And then I, I cry and a week passes.
I can't remember the pain, let's try again.
Lets feel that excitement.
Repeating weekly, more frequently.
And each time i'm running out of wishes,
Running out of chances.
I don't want to die.
I've already made plans for this book to be published, with or without
me on this earth.
This book is my baby,
And addiction for me is like giving birth.

Alcoholic

I remember less and less,
Each time I take a sip.
I now live in a foggy state,
Of fog and IV drips.
I think that it all started when,
My mental health declined.
I couldn't bear to think or feel,
So I left it behind.
I left behind my memories,
And personality.
I threw away all of the things,
The things that made me me.
I am an alcoholic,
I know that to be true.
Today I sit and simmer,
Feeling sad, sorry and blue.
If I don't change I will soon die,
Or forget who I am.
Won't even get to say goodbye,
I'm not a trusty man.
I want my mental function back,
And all that is good health.
And in spite of all that I lack,
I'll make of that my wealth.

Damage

I'm frightened and I feel alone,
Can't trust myself at all.
And my responsibility,
Well damn how far I fall.
I can't be what I need to be,
I can't take care of you.
And now it's time for me to change,
To be someone brand new.
I want to have a future,
I want to be of service.
But all I have I seem to light,
And throw into the furnace.
Sometimes I look at photographs,
Of when my eyes had light.
A time when I could laugh and love,
And sleep all through a night.
The last time that I almost died,
I thought of those who had.
I wondered, in their last moments,
Were they this scared and sad?
And that thought made me tremble,
I don't want to be next.
My life seems so uncertain now,
I'm foggy and perplexed.
I can't form a whole sentence,
Most days I am in bed.
Recovering from damage,
That I've done to my head.

Bite

I don't want your 'help'.
I'm already cowering in the corner,
Fighting for myself,
Desperately trying to survive.
And your hands grab at me,
Trying to usher me into a cage,
Whereby you can 'fix me'.
And when your hands get close,
I will bite. I will bite until you bleed.
Your idealistic views of therapy,
Your good intent. To hell with it!
To be left alone and to fight for myself,
That's all that sees me through.
And you would take that from me too.
You would take that from me too.
All my life I have been manhandled,
I have been beaten, been maimed.
And all in the name of kindness Sir,
All in its name.
I won't let you near me, I see through you,
See exactly what you're trying to do.
And I know as much as you do.
We both are mere humans, you are no God Sir.
Like a patient in Bedlam I rock with my chains,
Enslaved in the gesture of kindness,
No human rights, what are they to me now?
So an animal you see and that's what I will be for you.
Your good will is an illusion Sir, and I will destroy you.

Gods will

We all preach kindness,
We do try our best.
But without all the pain,
There would not be a test.
And maybe the Lord, as he planned the earth,
Knew that the suffering too has its worth.
It's ok to fail or do something bad,
To feel jealousy, anger, even to be sad.
Just pick yourself up and do better from now,
Follow your heart and it will show you how.
We love and we loathe our humanity,
Because we can't be what we wanted to be.
Accept in your journey, make peace with yourself,
Don't lose your own soul chasing women or wealth,
Or power or tricks; driven by your pain.
Hey you'll end up like me,
They say I am insane.
In this moment, be calm, take a breath and be still,
Succumb to your destiny, carved by Gods will.

Complicity

It's hard to see the wood from the trees,
When the world is built on illusions.
Born into a constructed world,
We're prone to some confusion.
It takes a certain set of skills,
To navigate our lives.
And when we get things wrong,
It cuts right through our flesh like knives.
Our brains are that of animals,
Our instinct's still intact.
On some level we must control,
How we behave and act.
But even those who fail this,
Are not just 'bad' or 'good'.
Some people make poor choices and,
Some are misunderstood.
There's no such thing as moral perfection,
Life can lead you in the wrong direction.
No man is above another,
That is another falsity.
Until we build an equal world,
We all have some complicity.

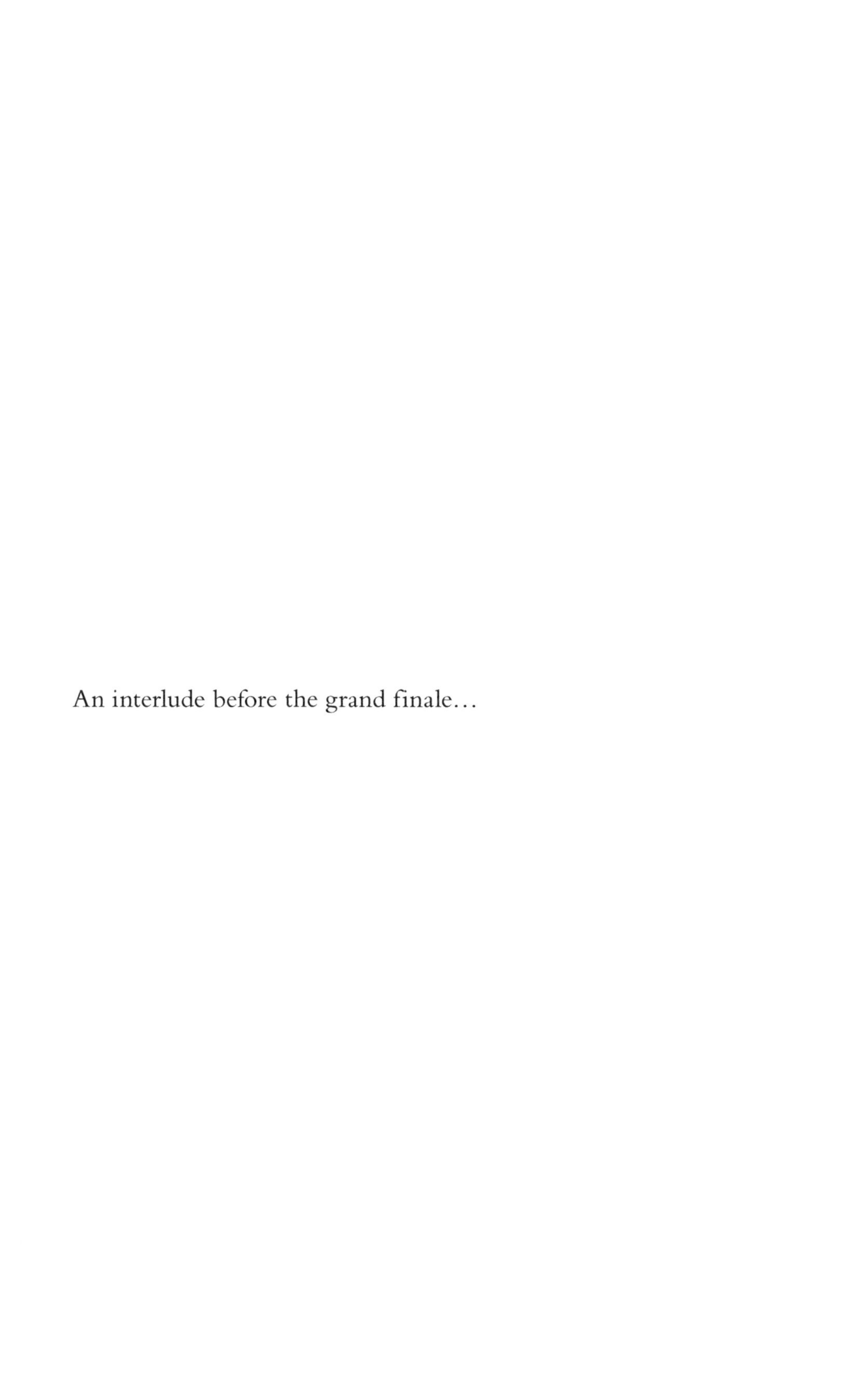

An interlude before the grand finale…

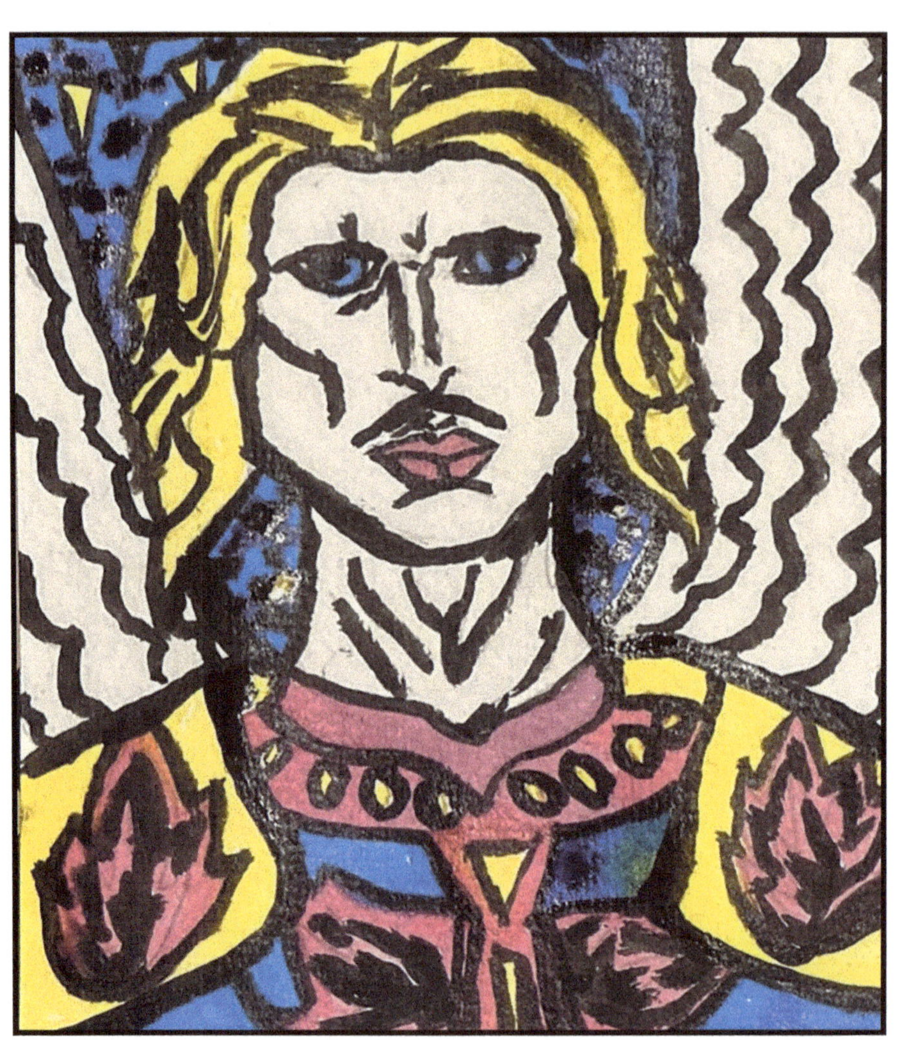

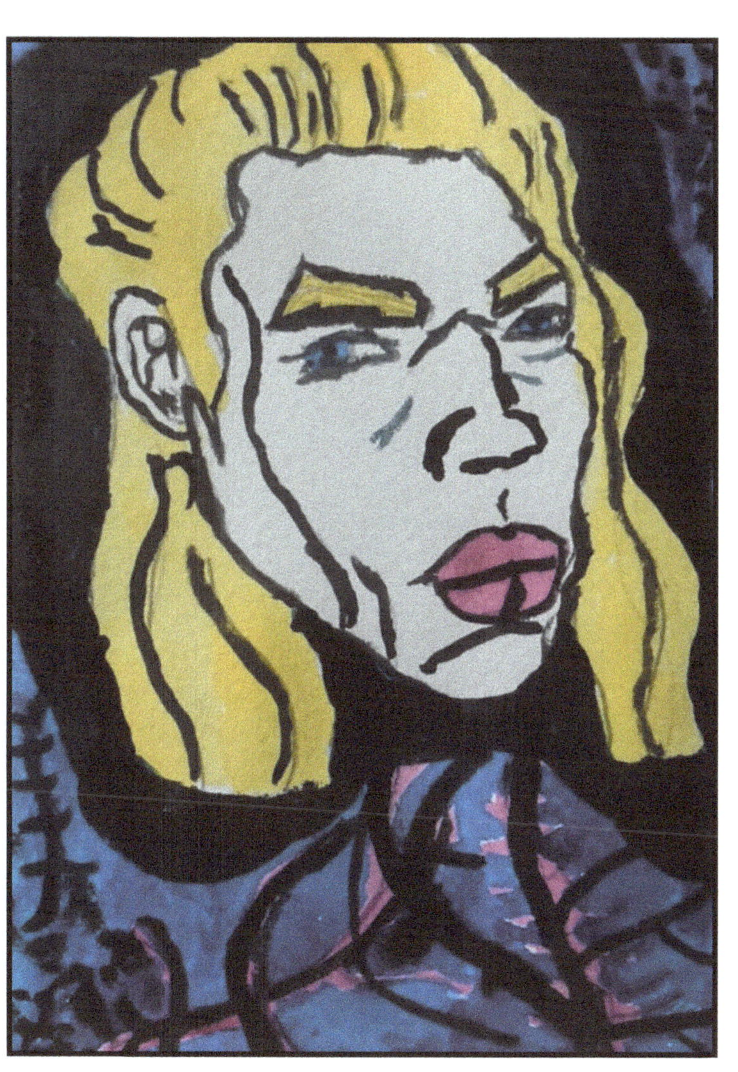

Friends

Oh, I say! It's not all bad.
But art is best made when I'm sad.
The friends I've met along the way,
Have influenced this man today.
Like mirrors to my deeper self,
And understanding mental health.
We'd have good laughs and vintage wine,
And mostly it was a swell time.
I fondly hold those years to me,
I felt at that time I was free.
Duty didn't call me then,
I soared the wind just like a Wren.
The ground a concept long forgot,
But even birds will die and rot.
It reached a time of change and new,
I reminisce on when I flew.
The parties, they were quite exquisite,
A bottle all that's requisite.
And still now If I choose it so,
It's all still there for me to go.
My loves! My fellow gentlemen,
I'm proud to have called you a friend.

Overwhelming emotion

Always I have felt the weight of the world,
I've carried it on my shoulders and it's proved a heavy burden.
To feel the suffering of every place and every time all at once.
And to be expected to live a carefree life.
Perhaps its shared consciousness or a task thrust forcefully into my
    hands.
A God decides that my trials are to be overwhelming emotion.
The confusion of growing up with the chaos inside of me,
Like hurricanes and fires they reap destruction.
'Be the good you want to see in the world', but where to start.
I ran away from it all, ran into oblivion so that I didn't have to recall.
This thing keeping me alive, this thing burning inside of me that I
    would deny.
Deny three times before the rooster crows.
But it never goes. Never goes.
So now I explore it, finally from an age of resignation,
And perhaps one of sadness, of grief.
I thought of talents I once possessed,
Speech, language, words.
Unrefined, undeveloped and unpractised,
But still I persevere.
For I stood at a crossroads where my life could only lead to two
    destinations.
One was the ground and one was the sky.
I must try at least or else I will die.

More

I sometimes willingly decide,
To sacrifice my soul.
To gain materialistic things,
Or to achieve a goal.
I know that I am sinning,
But I do so anyway.
I'd take my clothes off,
Lie me down,
And all to get some pay.
A part of me gets fainter,
Every thrust I disconnect.
But there is still a fraction,
Of my soul I will protect.
So long as some of it remains,
I can find some redemption.
And here and there I lend a hand,
In hopes of God's attention.
I want to live a wholesome life,
But the devil is seductive.
He tells me in this rotten world,
What I do is productive.
I know for certain when I die,
It's God that I will beg for.
But even when I try my best,
I still go back for more.

Alcohol

How absent you seem,
When you stumble down the street.
Wiping your mouth, the alcohol droplets transfer to your hand.
Your breath tastes sharp and bitter,
Your teeth uncleaned.
Your eyes are vacant and your brain is working on empty.
You feel adrenaline and sedation all at once,
And people stare and you don't even think of what they see.
Because it's not you that they're looking at,
Not anymore.
It's someone, something else.
There's nothing there in you,
You're on autopilot, which is the way home?
Is this how you want to live? Is this how you want to be seen?
You live inside a dream. A dream.
Wake up! It's time.
Stop running away because you are never hidden,
The world sees you in 20/20 vision.
They see your worst sides, your ugliest self,
And they believe it to be you.
They don't know what you can really do.

The jester and the swan

A trick of fools, and fools we are,
Performing for the king.
Dirty schemes and lawless means,
We dream we shall dethrone him.
And sat aside, the fairest face,
Intelligent and rare.
The swan of the blue bloodline,
With her looks so pure and fair.
Do we entertain you Miss?
An encore for your pleasure;
A smile from you, if you please,
Would be the richest treasure.
I've loved you from afar you see,
The sharpness of your mind.
And whilst I be a jester man,
I think we're like in kind.
It's funny, funny, frivolous,
Delirious caricature.
I'll have you breathing frantically,
As you cry out, 'more, more!'
A carnival carnality,
If you do feel the same.
I know our statuses don't match,
No need then, for my name.
And here we have, 'Jester, Jester!'
'I've loved you all this time',
'My swan can this be true or have you had too much red wine?'
'No sir, I assure you this, and hope you now can see;
You hit your head whilst juggling,
Hallucinating me!'

The wistful gentleman, revived

I said before that I was dying,
I meant it so sincerely.
I signed the end and dropped my pen,
Thinking life had beat me.
Well Sir, what a change of plans,
There's still more to be said,
And how I ask, can all that be,
If I were to be dead?
This wistful gentleman revived,
Relieved that I have just survived.
And here I am,
Expect to see,
More ballads from the bard that's me.
I stroke my locks of golden hair,
It seems i'm contemplating,
What the next book will entail,
And what I'll be creating.
I wink to those who share with me,
This piece of my dark soul.
In writing this, a part of me,
Is now becoming whole.

Fin…?